A Spider Might

Written and Illustrated by

Tom Walther

Sierra Club Books / Charles Scribner's Sons

San Francisco / New York

Copyright © 1978 by Tom Walther. All rights reserved.

No part of this book may be reproduced without the written consent of Sierra Club Books/Charles Scribner's Sons. Trade distribution is by Charles Scribner's Sons, 597 Fifth Avenue, New York, New York 10017.

A Spider Might was edited and prepared for publication at The Yolla Bolly Press, Covelo, California, under the supervision of James and Carolyn Robertson during the fall and winter of 1977. Production staff: Gene Floyd, Jay Stewart, Joyca Cunnan, Diana Fairbanks.

The Sierra Club, founded in 1892 by John Muir, has devoted itself to the study and protection of the nation's scenic and ecological resources — mountains, woodlands, wild shores and rivers. All Club publications are part of the nonprofit effort the Club carries on as a public trust. There are some 50 chapters coast to coast, in Canada, Hawaii and Alaska. Participation is invited in the Club's program to enjoy and preserve wilderness everywhere. Address: 530 Bush Street, San Francisco, California 94108.

Manufactured in the United States of America

1 3 5 7 9 11 13 15 17 19 MD/C 20 18 16 14 12 10 8 6 4 2
1 3 5 7 9 11 13 15 17 19 MD/P 20 18 16 14 12 10 8 6 4 2

Library of Congress Cataloging in Publication Data

Walther, Tom.
A spider might.

Bibliography: p. 140
Includes index.
SUMMARY: Describes the habits and characteristics of spiders and the natural
histories of twenty species commonly found in urban and suburban locations.
1. Spiders — Juvenile literature. [1. Spiders]
I. Title.
QL458.4.W34   595'.44   77-16474
ISBN 0-684-15588-5   ISBN 0-684-15592-3 pbk.

For Jane
with special thanks to
Sarah and my family

Table of Contents

Acknowledgments

This book would not have been possible without the aid of these more extensive works: *The World of Spiders* by W. S. Bristowe, *The Spider Book* by John H. Comstock, *American Spiders* by Willis J. Gertsch, and *A Guide to Spiders* by Herbert and Lorna Levi and Herbert Zim. All were used in the preparation of this book. Also invaluable were the works of Donald J. Borror and Richard E. White, Howard E. Evans, John H. Fabre, Frank Waters, and Norris McWhirter. A special thanks to Patrick Craig, the Spider Man of Berkeley, for sharing his beautiful slides, as well as his expertise as an arachnologist, and his inspiration.

This Book Is About Spiders

We see these small, eight-legged creatures in all sorts of places. Spiders live in holes, on walls, in trees, in grass, indoors, outdoors, everywhere. They are common, but at the same time they are a mystery to people. They are sometimes feared, but they play a useful and important part in life on the earth. They are of special interest to scientists because of their remarkable record of adaptation and survival. Because their actions are beyond the control of man, we have not bothered to study them with the same interest and concern we have applied to the study of creatures who do us harm, like boll weevils and aphids or give us something to sell, like bees and silkworms do.

Some people think spiders are creepy. Some people are afraid of spiders because a few species have a poisonous bite. Some people are afraid of spiders for no good reason at all. These people don't know very much about spiders, and they don't know what they are missing by being afraid. Most of the spiders in the world don't bite people. Instead, they help all of us by eating huge numbers of insects that might otherwise be a big problem. If you take an interest in spiders, there are fascinating discoveries in store for you. Are you ready?

In this book you will do some imagining about yourself and about spiders. You will see how amazing these fellow creatures really are. You will see how their bodies look. You will learn how they are named by scientists. And you will be introduced to some spiders that probably live very near where you are, right this minute.

About the Size of Spiders

The pictures in this book show most of the spiders larger than they actually are. The size of a spider's body (not including the legs) is given in millimeters (mm). There are about 25 mm in one inch; so 4 to 6 mm is about ¼ of an inch. The illustrations in the "Spiders to Find" section have a black silhouette showing the spider's actual size. If there is no silhouette, the drawing itself shows the actual size of the spider. When you come across unusual words referring to parts of a spider's body, look at the section called "Spider Body Parts" beginning on page 114 for some help.

Spider
Speculations

If you hunted and hunted
through all the books,
do you think you could find one
that could claim we humans
have been walking the earth
for 300 million years?
I don't think so,
but that long ago
a spider lived and died
and left a message.

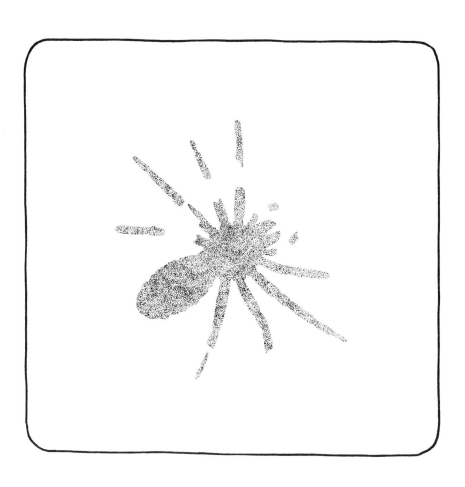

A spider fossil (an imprint in stone) dating from the Devonian period, 300 *million* years ago, was found near Aberdeen, Scotland. This earliest known spider is called *Palaeocteniza crassipes* Hirst. The oldest remains of *Homo sapiens* (that's us) date from only 300 to 450 *thousand* years ago.

If you become bored
with living in your town,
you might move to the country
and live in the shade of a leaf.
For food you could pounce on flies
as they came by.
You think you wouldn't?
There is a spider
who lives just this way.

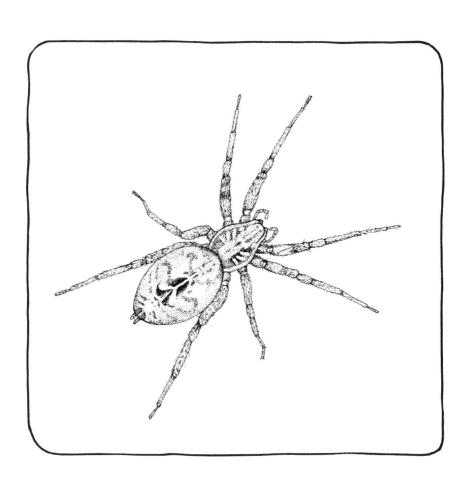

The Buzzing Spider, *Anyphaena accentuata,* lives among leaves and twigs and pounces on small flies and leafhoppers for food. When courting a female, the male vibrates his abdomen and makes a buzzing sound. The pale yellow to white colored *Anyphaena* spiders also live in grass and bushes, under logs, and in forest floor litter. *Anyphaena accentuata* is an English spider, but members of the genus *Anyphaena* also live in all parts of the United States. They grow to be from 4 to 6 mm in length.

Do you think
you would have the strength
to leap 20 times your body's length?
Try it. It is quite a distance.
In 1968, Robert Beamon jumped 29 feet, 2½ inches
in the long jump.
His jump is the world's record!
That distance is about 5 times his body's length!
But some spiders can do better.

This Zebra Spider, *Salticus scenicus,* is a member of a large family of Jumping Spiders called the Salticidae. It is found throughout the Northern Hemisphere and lives in houses and other buildings. The Zebra Spider is brown and white, and it grows to about 6 mm.

Instead of building webs, members of the spider family Salticidae stalk their prey like a cat and pounce on it. When frightened, the champion jumper, *Sitticus saltator,* can jump 20 times its own length.

Can you imagine sprouting plumes?
You would be an amazing sight.
You could wear them in parades
or wave them to get attention.
You could use them to signal friends
or to dust the living room.
You don't grow them,
but some spiders do.

Many Jumping Spiders, like this male *Phidippus audax,* have plumed legs and palps which they wave to attract a mate. This spider is usually found on plants and stones and sometimes in houses. He grows to a size of about 13 mm and is found from the Atlantic Coast states west to the Rocky Mountains.

When you need to travel a long distance,
wouldn't it be handy
if you could let out some threads
to catch the wind
and be lifted into flight?
If you were to try it,
you might find that
you are too heavy to fly
dangling on a thread in the wind.
But some spiders travel this way.

Some spiders can sail on threads of their own silk for long distances. This is called *ballooning,* and spiders belonging to the family called Linyphiidae are especially good at it. They stand with their abdomens raised and squirt out threads into rising air currents (usually on warm fall days after cool clear nights) and are lifted into flight. Some ballooning spiders have been found floating as high as 14,000 feet and have been met by ships hundreds of miles out at sea. But most ballooning spiders do not go higher than a few hundred feet in the air.

Would you like to go trapping
and use a sticky glob
on the end of a string
to catch your food?
When your prey came by,
you could drop or throw the glob
and stick your line to it,
then pull it in.
There is a spider that hunts this way.

The Bolas Spider, *Mastophora bisaccata,* is found in the southeastern United States. It captures passing moths by throwing out a sticky globule on a silk line. The Bolas Spider is a yellow brown color and can grow to about 14 mm. It is related to the orb-web weavers but has lost the ability to build webs.

If you had special glands
for making silk,
this ability would be useful.
You could make your own clothing
or ropes or belts or silk hats,
maybe even a parachute.
But you can't make silk —
a spider can.

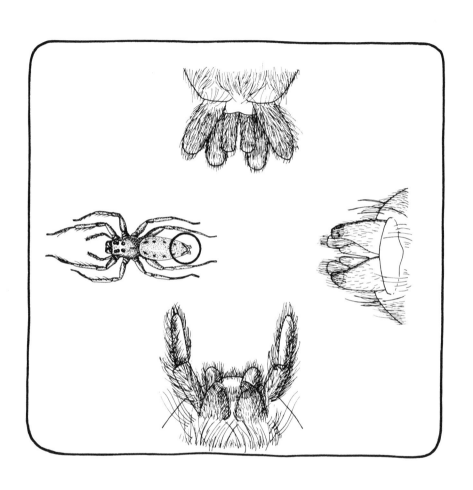

A spider may have five or six different types of silk glands that produce silk for different purposes. The spinnerets (shown here) are located at the back of the abdomen. Each spinneret contains spinning tubes from which silk is expelled. Some spiders may have a hundred or more of these tubes on one spinneret. The silk of the spider *Nephila clavipes* is the strongest natural fiber known. A spider's silk starts as a liquid which dries immediately in the air to make the strands we see.

Imagine tasting by touch!
You could sample foods at the store.
You could know ahead of time
which things you wouldn't want in your mouth.
You could take taste hikes
and know the flavors of all kinds of things:
rocks, trees, people.
We can't taste by touching,
but a spider might!

Spiders have taste glands in their gullets, but they can also taste by touching. The taste-by-touch or *chemotactic* sense is located in their palps and legs. It protects them from eating bad-tasting prey. This sense also protects bad-tasting creatures from being injured by a spider.

You have grown bigger and bigger
since your birth.
Would you grow better,
if you slipped out of your skin
and grew a new larger one?
Changing skins this way would look odd
and be hard to do.
This thought may give you the chills.
You wouldn't do it,
but a spider might.

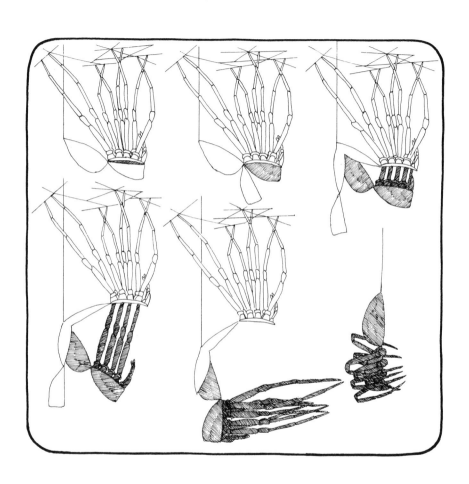

What if some joker
pulls off your leg?
Could you grow a new one?
You could have a wooden leg made
or walk on crutches.
Spiders have a useful ability
for just such situations!

If a spider is caught by a leg, the leg will break off at a weak spot just below the coxa (the upper segment of a spider's leg). A new leg begins to grow in the coxa and uncoils in the next moult. It takes three or four moults before it catches up in size with the spider's other legs. Spiders can also regenerate *or* grow new maxillae, chelicerae, and spinnerets.

Someday if you marry
and decide to become a parent,
would you have 2,292 children?
How would you feed them?
Where would you all live?
Who would do the dishes?
For human parents,
this is an impossible number
of children to have,
but a spider couple might!

If you were stranded without water
for more than a few days,
life would become very uncomfortable.
Two weeks or a month
without any water at all
would be fatal for us.
But some spiders have adapted
to survive for a long time without water.

Some spiders, including several common house spiders, can live for months without water. This spider is a female *Herpyllus vasifer*. She lives as a wandering hunter and is found in the eastern United States between boards, under stones, and in dark crevices. Her body is black with pink or white markings along the back.

If you had to travel
from one tree to another,
would you walk on a bridge
made of a thread?
You would be better off to climb down
and use the ground.
But many spiders have a way
to bridge the gap.

Spiders often use a thread as a bridge to get from one plant to another. The spider stands in one spot and lets out a thread for the wind to carry until it snags on another spot. Then the spider draws this thread tight and uses it to travel. The spider strengthens the bridge by adding a silk dragline each time it crosses.

If one day while climbing in
and swinging through trees,
you saw Miss Muffet below
eating her curds and whey,
would you swing down
and give her a scare?
Though you wouldn't
or certainly shouldn't,
a spider might!

Little Miss Muffet — whose real name was Patience — may have been frightened by spiders, but her father, Dr. Thomas Muffet, enjoyed their company. He studied and wrote about spiders in England, in the late 1500s. Their webs draped the rooms of his house. Dr. Muffet thought spiders could be used as cures for most illnesses. He believed spiders in a house helped to keep away gout, and he gave Patience spiders to swallow as pills when she was ill.

The belief that spiders could prevent or cure fevers was common in ancient times and even up to the nineteenth century. People ate them like pills, or carried them in nutshells hung around the neck as charms, or just allowed them to remain around the house. Spider webs have often been used as a dressing for wounds.

Suppose you did not have ears.
Would the hairs on your legs
pick up sounds?
They might tickle when you sang
or talked or walked past a radio.
You might have to put your leg on the table
at dinner to hear the conversation!
Fortunately we don't hear
with the hairs on our legs,
but some spiders do.

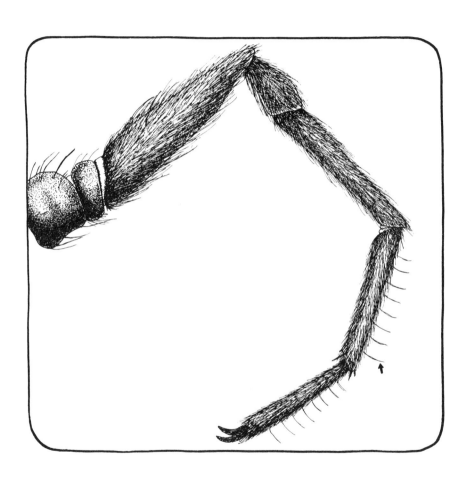

The trichobotheria are hairlike organs on a spider's legs which can sense wind and web movements as well as the vibrations in the air that we hear as sound.

If cockroaches became
pests in your home,
you could find it hard
to put up a fight.
They hide in places
where you can't get to them,
but a spider might.

The Huntsman Spider, *Heteropoda venatoria,* is a valued guest in tropical houses because it catches and eats cockroaches. It is yellow brown in color and grows to 24 mm.

Except for a few who prefer to eat other spiders, all spiders are insect eaters. They are welcomed and valued all over the world by people who recognize that these small creatures help protect their gardens and houses from being overrun by hungry insects. Spiders can catch insects in places and ways that are just not possible for man to do.

Would it be any fun
to spend your life
on a vertical wall,
hanging from cracks
by your fingers and toes?
How would you sit, sleep,
read, or write?
Some spiders spend their lives this way.

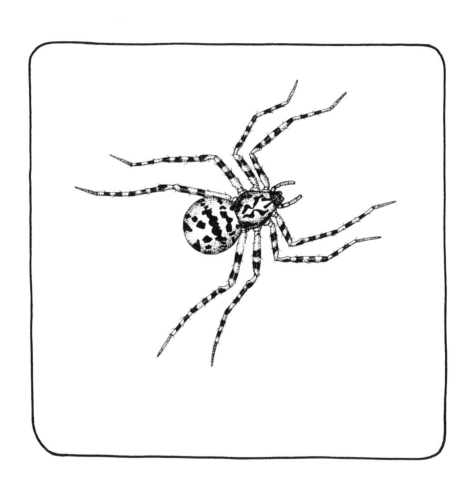

The Spitting Spider, *Scytodes thoracica,* spends her life slowly walking walls in search of food. When she finds an insect, she moves close enough to spit a sticky gum which binds her victim to the wall. These yellow and black spiders are mostly tropical and grow to 8 mm.

If you left a thread
everywhere you went,
you would get exhausted
and use up a lot of thread too.
Streets and sidewalks
would be jungles of thread.
Houses and stores
would soon be filled.
Would it really make sense for you
to continually leave a thread behind?
For most spiders it does.

Most spiders make and lay out a silk thread for use as a life line when they travel. They attach this line or dragline to the surface they are walking on with special attachment disks so that they never have far to fall. Sometimes a male spider will follow the dragline left by a female as a way to locate a mate.

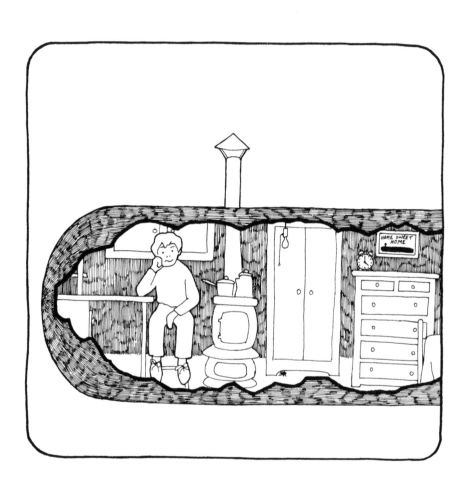

Would you live alone
in a tube with no door
for almost your entire life?
Would you like to do it?
You could not jump or run.
You'd have no visitors, no friends,
just the same curved walls.
You might be bored with such a life.
There are some spiders who live this way.

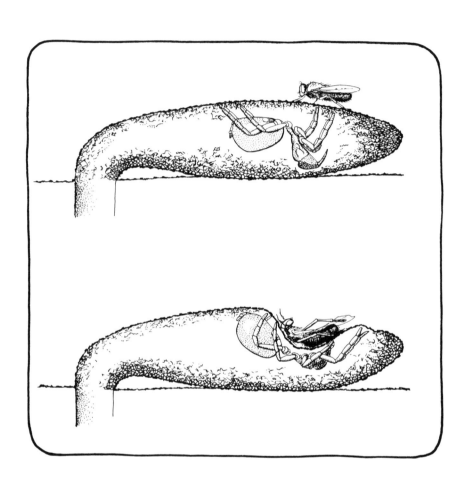

Atypus affinis, the European Purseweb Spider, normally spends its entire adult life inside a silk and sand tube. Part of the tube is above ground and looks like a root. When an insect walks across the outside of the tube, the spider bites through the tube with its long fangs and poisons the insect. Then it cuts a slit in the tube and pulls the victim in to eat, throws out the remains, and sews up the slit from the inside.

In North America, *Atypus bicolor* lives in a hole dug at the base of a tree in a fingerlike tube that may extend six inches up the side of the tree. This spider lives east of the Mississippi River and as far north as New England.

When you are hungry
and your mother is away,
do you ever have thoughts
of eating your sisters and brothers?
You could not eat them.
It would not be polite!
You wouldn't even try to.
But a spider might!

Some mother spiders feed their young, but many leave their children to provide for themselves. Young spiders, when left without food, will eat each other. The practice of spiders eating spiders is common even among adults. In fact, the spider is the number one enemy of other spiders. Because of this habit, it is not possible to raise the large quantities of spiders necessary to produce spider silk commercially, like people do with silkworms.

Would you like to have
more than two eyes?
Imagine eight!
Perhaps you could see to the front
and someone sneaking up from behind,
the sky above and your feet below,
even to the sides,
all at one time!
That could make you dizzy.
Picture all those eyes on your face.
What a sight!
Eight is too many for you,
but for some spiders, just right.

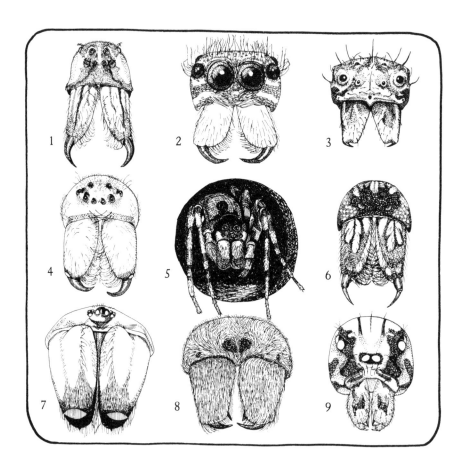

Most spiders have eight eyes, some have six, and a few, which live underground, don't have any. The smiling faces shown here have either six or eight eyes. These faces belong to members of the following families:

1. Pisauridae, Nursery Web Spiders
2. Salticidae, Jumping Spiders
3. Thomisidae, Crab Spiders
4. Heteropodidae, Giant Crab Spiders
5. Lycosidae, Burrowing Wolf Spiders
6. Anyphaenidae, Buzzing Spiders
7. Atypidae, Purse Web Spiders
8. Eresidae, Lace Web Spiders
9. Scytodidae, Spitting Spiders

When frost appears in autumn,
would you climb up and hang
like a plaque on a wall?
Could you bend your legs back
and hang there
day after day,
until warmer weather came?
There is a spider
who spends each winter this way.

When frosts come in the fall and early winter, the spider *Pholcus* takes a rigid posture pressed tight against the wall with its legs bent back in an odd way. It remains this way until warmer days return. *Pholcus* or Daddy Longlegs is a house spider. When it is alarmed, it whirls around and shakes its web. This has the effect of making both the spider and the web appear invisible.

Could you sit down one day
and eat as much as you weigh?
That's a lot of food
for one day!
So much food stuffed into you
would make you sick,
but a spider might find it possible.

Some spiders can eat as much as their own weight in a single day, if they can catch that much food. When food is not available, some spiders can go for long periods without eating. Certain desert spiders can survive for six months, and some tarantulas can live for two years without a meal.

You probably would not choose
to live in an outhouse.
It would be too small.
There could be an odor problem!
For you an outhouse
wouldn't be the best home,
but some spiders find it ideal!

Cobweb Spiders often enjoy life in a web built in a cozy corner of an outhouse. Here they can catch flies and other insects. This Cobweb Weaver is a female *Steatoda bipunctata*. Members of the genus *Steatoda* live throughout the United States.

On a hot summer day
it would be convenient
to stay underwater
for long, cool hours.
Could you haul
down in your hair
the air you would need to breathe?
Some special spiders do.

Certain spiders which live near water will run down a stem into the water to hide from an enemy. They breathe from an air bubble that forms around their body hair. Some can stay underwater as long as ten hours. This spider is a male *Pirata piraticus,* a Wolf Spider. He lives in swamps.

Spider Parts
and
Names

Spider Body Parts

These diagrams show a spider's body with the different parts pointed out and named. They will help you understand the descriptions of spiders in this book and help you to see how spiders look.

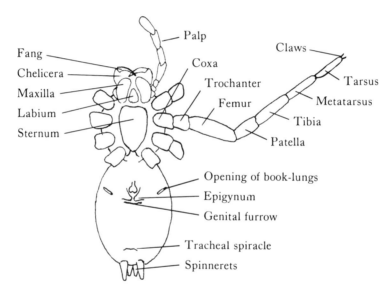

LOOKING AT THE BOTTOM

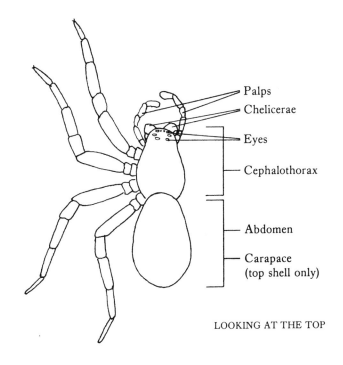

Palps
Chelicerae
Eyes
Cephalothorax
Abdomen
Carapace
(top shell only)

LOOKING AT THE TOP

Some of the parts have names that look big and impossible. If you sound them out slowly, these names are pronounceable, and you can enjoy the sounds they make. Look these pictures over. Maybe you can find some of the words you stumbled on earlier and learn what they refer to.

115

Spider Names

Scientists throughout the world have agreed upon a system for classifying and naming living things. The system was developed by Carolus Linnaeus in the 1700s and is based mostly on the way creatures are built. All the names are made up of Latin words. This system makes it easy for all scientists to know what plant or animal another scientist is talking about, even if that scientist is in another part of the world.

It works by dividing living things into smaller and smaller groups, like dividing a pie into smaller and smaller pieces. The first cut divides the living things of the world into two kingdoms: Plantae (plants) and Animalia (animals). Spiders are members of the kingdom Animalia; so are people, birds, insects, reptiles, fish, and other creatures. Trees, flowers, and vegetables are members of the plant kingdom.

The kingdoms are divided into phyla. There are more than 20 phyla in the animal kingdom. Spiders belong to the phylum Arthropoda; so do insects, crayfish, centipedes, and others. All Arthropoda wear their skeletons outside and have jointed legs. Why aren't people arthropods?

The phyla are then divided into classes. Spiders belong to the class Arachnida; so do mites, ticks, scorpions, harvestmen, and a few other creatures. All Arachnida have the head and thorax in one segment called the cephalothorax (you can find a picture of it in "Spider Body Parts," pages 114-115). Arachnids lack wings and antennae. They have four pairs of legs and a pair of palps.

The classes are divided into orders. Spiders are of the order Araneae. Araneae is another word for spider. All members of this order have a body divided into a cephalothorax and a short, usually unsegmented, abdomen. The chelicerae are modified into poison fangs. All Spiders have leglike palps, simple eyes, a silk-making apparatus at the end of their abdomen, and lung sacs or tracheae (breathing tubes) in the abdomen.

The order Araneae is further divided into families. B. J. Kaston, in his book *How to Know the Spiders,* recognizes 53 families of American spiders.

The families are then divided into genera and the genera into species. When the scientific name of a particular plant or animal is given, it is usually the genus and species. The genus is capitalized, the species is not. People are of the genus *Homo* and the species *sapiens,* or *Homo sapiens.* This name refers to all the people on earth — even you, since we all have the same structure and basic genetic makeup.

The classification of the Zebra Spider on page 23 would look like this:

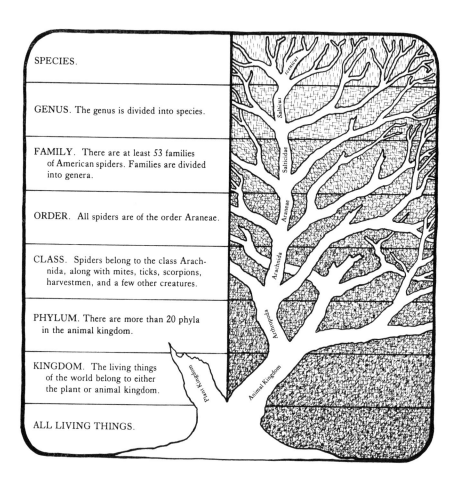

SPECIES.

GENUS. The genus is divided into species.

FAMILY. There are at least 53 families of American spiders. Families are divided into genera.

ORDER. All spiders are of the order Araneae.

CLASS. Spiders belong to the class Arachnida, along with mites, ticks, scorpions, harvestmen, and a few other creatures.

PHYLUM. There are more than 20 phyla in the animal kingdom.

KINGDOM. The living things of the world belong to either the plant or animal kingdom.

ALL LIVING THINGS.

118

Kingdom: Animalia
Phylum: Arthropoda
Class: Arachnida
Order: Araneae
Family: Salticidae
Genus: *Salticus*
Species: *scenicus*

When we write about a spider, we use the family name or the genus and species names. To tell these names apart remember that the family name is capitalized and ends with the letters "dae," the genus is capitalized also, but it is in *italics* too. The species is never capitalized, but it is in italics.

This system may seem complicated, but if you think about it, it is basically very simple, once you learn what all those words mean! That's the hardest part. We use similar systems for telephone numbers and zip codes (these use numbers instead of words) or to address letters. We divide large groups into smaller and smaller groups until we get just who we want to talk to or our letter gets to the right door and person. You could invent a system that works this way for classifying the people in your class or on your block, or the kinds of buildings in your town, or almost anything. Think of some other systems of classification you use every day.

119

Looking
for
Spiders

Would you like to find some spiders, just to see what a real cephalothorax looks like? You can begin by looking almost anywhere. Members of the order Araneae choose a wide variety of habitats. The best place to start, especially in warm weather, is outdoors. Look in shrubs, on trees, in grass, in leaves, under junk, under windowsills, in abandoned buildings, in barns, or even in holes in the ground. If you find a web, it is often an indication that its builder is nearby. Indoors you may notice a spider strolling across your wall or floor. They may be found in corners, cellars, basements, and in all sorts of cracks.

When you find spiders stuck in the bathtub or sink, you can give them a lift to a safer location with a piece of paper. It might be easier to wash them down the drain, but many old stories say that killing a spider brings bad luck and helping them brings good.

The webs of spiders come in some basic types that you can easily identify. The orderly wheellike web you often see pictured with lines radiating from a central hub and other lines connecting in a spiral from ray to ray is called an *orb web*. A *cobweb* is an irregular net made of a mass of threads going in all directions. You may see it often in indoor corners.

A *sheet web* is a more or less closely woven sheet of threads going in all directions across a single plane. Because of the closeness of the strands of silk, a sheet web often has a milky white color. The *funnel web* is a sheet web with a tube near the edge or sometimes an opening elsewhere into the sheet. The spider waits in this tube for insects to walk across or fall onto the sheet, then it runs out to capture them.

Once you have found spiders, you can watch them grow and check back to see how and what they are doing over a period of time. Since spiders are small, a hand lens or magnifying glass can be a useful tool to help you see their beauty close-up. A pad of paper and a pencil for drawing and writing about what you see will help you remember and share what you have observed.

Poisonous Spiders

All spiders have poison fangs. That is how spiders kill their prey, but in North America only two types are considered dangerous to man. One of these is the Black Widow of the genus *Latrodectus,* and there are three species covered by the common name of Black Widow. The Brown Recluse or Violin Spider, *Loxosceles reclusa,* is not as well known or found in as many places as the Widows, but they can also have a serious bite.

Spiders, even the ones mentioned above, are timid and would rather escape than attack a person. They bite only when they are frightened or molested, but it is a good idea to approach any creature you don't know with respect and caution.

The Black Widows are members of the cobweb-weaving Theridiidae family. They are coal black with red, or yellow, or red and yellow markings. The most constant mark is the red hourglass shape on the bottom of the abdomen. The female, who sits in her web and does not wander, may have red marks along her back and over the spinnerets. These spots can be different in size and number on each Black Widow Spider. Sometimes there are no spots at all. The male, which is about half the size of the female, is usually marked with more color.

Black Widows are found near houses and other buildings, in trash and dumps, and under objects of many sorts. They spend their lives mostly in their webs, but the males do go wandering in search of a mate. The males do not feed or bite at this time.

If you were to receive a bite from a Black Widow, you would feel severe abdominal pain and pain in the muscles of your feet, but there would be no swelling at the place where you were bitten. Saliva would flow freely for a while, then your mouth would be dry. You would sweat a lot and your eyelids would become swollen. The bite of a Black Widow is rarely fatal and in most cases the victim recovers after a few painful days. An antivenin is not in common use in the United States, but a doctor can give a shot to relieve the muscle pain.

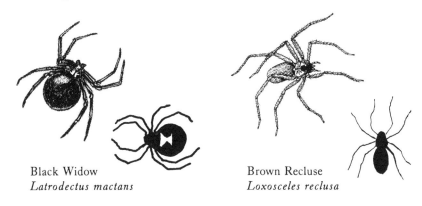

Black Widow
Latrodectus mactans

Brown Recluse
Loxosceles reclusa

The Brown Recluse, *Loxosceles reclusa,* is a member of the family Scytodidae and lives in Texas, Kansas, Missouri, and Oklahoma. This yellow brown spider with a violin-shaped mark on its cephalothorax lives in houses on the floor or behind furniture. It sometimes rests in clothing and towels and through these articles comes into contact with people.

If you were to receive a bite from one of these spiders, there might be no harm at all. In more severe cases the actual bite may sting slightly, but the main symptoms would appear six to eight hours later. A red zone appears around the bite, then a crust begins to form. The victim experiences chills, fever, and nausea. Beginning about the second day, the tissue or flesh in the area of the bite starts to die. The skin breaks and a scab forms, but the wound is slow to heal. In some cases liver and/or kidney damage may occur, and this may eventually cause the death of the victim. In the event of a bite from a spider known to be poisonous, it is a good idea to see a doctor right away.

Large Spiders

In the southwestern United States, we have a few of the large spiders we commonly call tarantulas. This *Aphonopelma chalcodes,* a member of the family Theraphosidae, is found in New Mexico, Arizona, and Southern California. It may grow to a length of 70 mm. This ground-dwelling spider hides in natural holes and other niches during the day and does its hunting at night. The hair on this large spider's abdomen comes off easily and is irritating to human skin. But its bite is no more harmful than a bee sting. Some females of this species may live to be 20 years old.

Tarantula (actual size)
Aphonopelma chalcodes

Another large spider lives in a tube in the ground with a hinged trapdoor at the top. Members of the family Ctenizidae live in most of the southern states of the United States. This spider, called *Bothriocyrtum californicum,* lives in its tube

128

built into sunny hillsides in Southern California. By using a spiny rake on their jaws, these spiders dig their tubelike burrows. The tube, including the opening, is lined with silk; then the spider cuts around the rim of the opening, except for a part left for a hinge. The top of the lid is camouflaged with debris, and additional silk is added under the lid to make it fit tight. The spider waits in its tube with the door closed until it feels the vibration of a passing prey. It then runs out, catches the victim, and hauls it into the tube to eat. The female rarely leaves her tube except to catch prey. The adult male leaves to go wandering in search of a mate.

Trapdoor Spider
Bothriocyrtum californicum

Spiders to Find

If you look closely at a small white or yellow white sheet web that you find under windowsills, in corners, and over cracks, underneath it you may see a spider of the Oecobiidae family, like this *Oecobius annulipes*. This small spider waits in a tube or on a small web beneath the larger web for prey to come by. It has a pale yellow cephalothorax with black lines around the edge and an abdomen that is white or light brown with many dark spots.

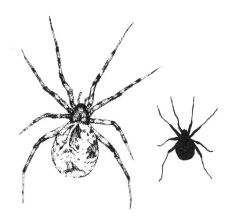

Oecobius annulipes

American House Spider
Achaearanea tepidariorum

The female *Achaearanea tepidariorum* (on page 130) is a very common house spider. She builds a cobweb. Her cephalothorax is yellow brown, and her abdomen can vary from dirty white to brown. Females have yellow legs while the males' legs are orange. This spider is found standing on her web which she builds in the corners of barns and houses and also outside, under stones and boards or on buildings and fences. This spider has a special comb on the last segment (the tarsus) of her fourth pair of legs. She uses these combs for flinging silk over prey that is tangled in her web.

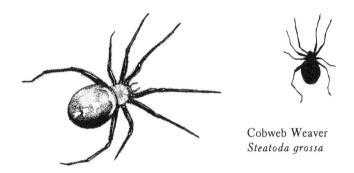

Cobweb Weaver
Steatoda grossa

Another common house spider of the family Theridiidae is this spider, *Steatoda grossa*. The female shown here has a brown carapace and a dark purple brown abdomen with pale yellow markings. The abdomen is oval shaped. *Steatoda*

131

grossa is a cobweb builder and a common house spider throughout the world. It may live as long as six years and is reported to prey on Black Widows.

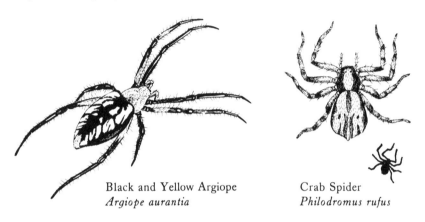

Black and Yellow Argiope
Argiope aurantia

Crab Spider
Philodromus rufus

You may notice this large, brightly colored spider in a sunny place like your garden. *Argiope aurantia* has a carapace covered with silvery hairs. Her abdomen is black and yellow, pointed behind, and notched at the front to form a hump on each side. She sits in the center of her web on a heavy, zigzag band of silk called a stabilimentum. This spider builds its web in gardens, around houses, and in tall grass.

The Crab Spider, *Philodromus rufus,* lives on plants and sometimes indoors on the ceilings of houses in all but the very southern part of the United States. It can run very fast and has a flat body which allows it to get into cracks. This spider is red and yellow with white rings around its eyes. Because of its protective coloring, it is difficult to see, except when moving.

The genus *Araneus* contains more species than any other genus of spiders. There are some 1,500 species of these orb-web builders throughout the world.

This spider, *Araneus trifolium,* is know as the Shamrock Spider. Its carapace has one black stripe down the middle and one to each side. The abdomen may be pale green, brown, or grey, or even a purple red, but it always has the

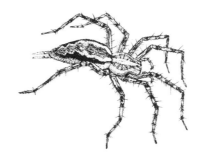

Shamrock Spider
Araneus trifolium

Grass Spider
Agelenopsis pennsylvanica

same pattern of white spots. The male's abdomen is yellow or white. This spider makes an orb web. Above and to one side of the web, the Shamrock Spider makes a hiding place in a folded leaf or in a bunch of leaves. Vibrations from the web are transmitted to the spider by a special line attached to the hub of the web. You can find these webs in tall grass.

Spiders of the genus *Agelenopsis,* like *Agelenopsis pennsylvanica* (on page 133) are Funnel Weavers and may be most easily found in late summer when the morning dew shimmers on their webs in lawns. The spider hides at the narrow end of the funnel which spreads out across the grass. When it feels the vibration of an insect walking across its web, the spider runs out, bites the insect, and takes it back to the funnel to eat. Its long, jointed spinnerets are used to spread silk as the spider adds new layers to the sheet web.

You can sometimes find the funnel webs of *Tegenaria domestica* in dark, moist places such as cellars, under stones, and in rock crevices. Males and females may live in the same web for two or three months during the breeding season. The cephalothorax of this spider is pale yellow with two grey stripes, and the abdomen has a number of grey spots. The long-legged *Tegenaria domestica* is found throughout the world. It was once believed that malaria, a tropical disease, could be cured by swallowing this spider.

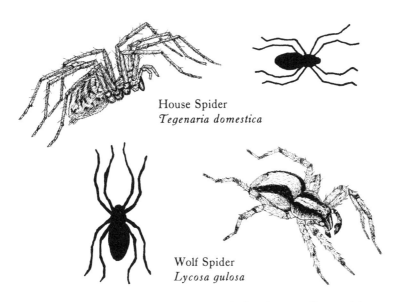

House Spider
Tegenaria domestica

Wolf Spider
Lycosa gulosa

Lycosa gulosa is a member of the family Lycosidae, commonly called the Wolf Spiders. They are found in the United States and Canada, running over dead leaves on the forest floor. They are dark brown with grey markings on the carapace and black on the abdomen. Instead of building a web, they wander in search of food. The female *Lycosa* carries her eggs in a spherical egg sac attached to her spinnerets. After the young emerge, they climb on their mother's abdomen. She carries them this way for some time.

This very small spider, *Ostearius melanopygius,* is a member of the family Linyphiidae. It is brown and makes a small sheet web. It can be found throughout the world among dead leaves, under stones, and in or on vegetation. It may grow to a length of 1.5 mm. The Linyphiidae, also known as the Dwarf Spiders, are very numerous, but very little is known about them because they are small and difficult to observe. As a group they consume a great number of insects. The web of these spiders consists of an irregular section above and a platform of silk underneath on which the spider sits.

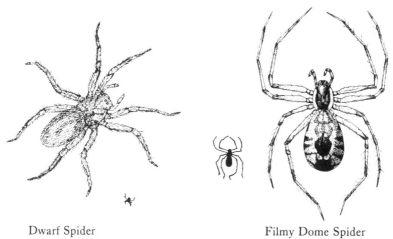

Dwarf Spider
Ostearius melanopygius

Filmy Dome Spider
Prolinyphia marginata

136

The spider *Prolinyphia marginata* is a member of a subfamily of the Linyphiidae called Linyphiinae. They are larger than the Dwarf Spiders. The carapace on this spider is longer than it is wide, and it is a dark brown color with white markings toward the edges. The abdomen is widest and highest toward the rear and has brown markings on a yellow white background. Its web is found in shrubs, and sometimes a male and female hang upside down in the same web. If an insect gets caught in the web, the spider bites the prey from below and pulls it through the sheet and wraps it up. The web protects the spider against enemies coming from above, and sometimes a second sheet of web provides protection from below.

The Pirate Spiders, like the *Ero furcata* (on page 138), invade the webs of other spiders. It is possible that they prey only on other spiders and do not eat insects. *Ero furcata* is a slow-moving spider that bites its victim on the leg and so paralyzes it. It then sucks the victim dry by using the victim's leg like a straw. Sometimes this spider will sit with its legs outstretched under leaves and wait for passing spiders. It is light yellow with a dark, broad band on each side of its carapace. The abdomen is grey with brown spots and is as high as it is long and has two humps. *Ero furcata* is found in damp places under stones and leaves.

137

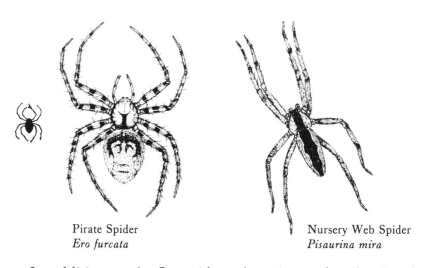

Pirate Spider
Ero furcata

Nursery Web Spider
Pisaurina mira

In addition to the Lycosidae, there is another family of hunting spiders called the Pisauridae, or Nursery Web Spiders. The mother carries the young in a spherical sac like the Lycosidae, but shortly before the young are to emerge, she hangs the sac on some leaves and builds a netlike nursery web around it and guards the young in their nursery.

This *Pisaurina mira* is yellow to light brown with a wide darker brown band down the middle of the carapace and abdomen. The band is edged with white on the abdomen. *Pisaurina mira* lives in tall grass and bushes in the eastern part of the United States.

This *Geolycosa missouriensis,* a Burrowing Wolf Spider, spends most of its life in a burrow in the ground. It waits at the mouth of the burrow for prey. This spider is hard to observe because it is sensitive to ground vibrations and hides in its burrow when it senses danger. To see one, you must wait quietly by the burrow for a few minutes until the spider comes back to the surface. This kind of spider lives in sandy areas of the United States from the East Coast to as far west as Arizona and Utah.

Burrowing Wolf Spider
Geolycosa missouriensis

Jumping Spider
Phidippus clarus

This spider is a Jumping Spider, *Phidippus clarus.* It is active during the day and likes sunshine. At night this spider stays in a little silk cocoon or finds a crevice. *Phidippus clarus* is found throughout the United States on plants. It is the most widely distributed member of its genus. The female is yellow orange to brown and has black and white markings. The male has a black cephalothorax, and his abdomen has a broad black band down the middle with red stripes to the sides. He also has a white band around the base of the abdomen and often several pairs of white spots at the edges of the black band.

The Jumping Spiders have very good vision compared to other invertebrates (or animals without backbones). Many can see well enough to recognize prey at 100 to 200 mm, and some can change the color of their eyes.

Books About Spiders

There are more secrets in the spider world than can ever be put in one book. If you enjoy looking at spiders, you can find more information about them in these books.

Bristowe, W. S. *The World of Spiders*. The New Naturalist. Rev. ed. London: Collins, 1976. This book from England has interesting accounts of the lives of many spiders. Mr. Bristowe has a sense of humor and love for spiders that makes the book fun. It is illustrated with drawings and photographs.

Comstock, John H. *The Spider Book*. Rev. ed. Ithaca, New York: Cornell University Press, Comstock Publishing Co., Inc., 1948. This useful older book has much good information, photographs, and illustrations. It is a book for the serious student.

Fabre, John H. *The Life of the Spider*. New York: Horizon Press, 1971. Mr. Fabre is a scientist-poet. He tells of the things he has discovered about spiders by watching them and of his experiments with them. The book is not illustrated, but it is great reading.

Gertsch, William J. *American Spiders*. Princeton, New Jersey: D. Van Nostrand Co., Inc., 1949. This book tells about the habits and lives of American and Canadian spiders. It is illustrated with both color and black and white photographs and diagrams.

Kaston, B. J. *How to Know the Spiders*. 2nd ed. Dubuque, Iowa: Wm. C. Brown and Co., 1972. Kaston's book is the most up-to-date book for the scientific identification of American spiders. This complete guide to spiders is for serious students of the spider world. It is illustrated.

Levi, Herbert W., Levi, Lorna R., and Zim, Herbert S. *A Guide to Spiders and Their Kin*. New York: Golden Press, 1968. This inexpensive book is loaded with color pictures of spiders and some of their relatives from all over the world. It gives good basic information and is a handy guide to spiders for the beginner.

Index

Dragline, 63, 83
Dwarf Spiders (family, Linyphiidae), 31, 136-137
Egg sac, *55*, 135, 138
Epigynum, 114
Eresidae (family, Lace Web Spiders), 95
Ero furcata (Pirate Spider), 137-138
European Purseweb Spider (*Atypus affinis*), 87
Eyes, *95*, 115
Family, 117
Fangs, 114
Femur, 114
Funnel Weavers, 134
Funnel web, 124
Genus, genera, 116-119
Geolycosa missouriensis (Burrowing Wolf Spider), 139
Giant Crab Spiders (family, Heteropodidae), 95
Herpyllus vasifer, 59
Heteropoda venatoria (Huntsman Spider), 75
Heteropodidae (family, Giant Crab Spiders), 95
Homo sapiens, 15, 117
Huntsman Spider (*Heteropoda venatoria*), 75
Jumping Spiders (family, Salticidae), 23, 27, 95, 139-140
Kingdom, 116
Labium, 114
Lace Web Spiders (family,

Eresidae), 95
Latrodectus mactans (Black Widow), 124-126, 132
Linnaeus, Carolus, 116
Linyphiidae (family, Dwarf Spiders), 31, 136
Linyphiinae (subfamily, Sheet Web Weavers), 137
Loxosceles reclusa (Brown Recluse), 124, 126-127
Lycosa gulosa (Wolf Spider), 135
Lycosidae (family, Wolf Spiders), 95, 111, 135, 138, 139
Mastophora bisaccata (Bolas Spider), 35
Maxilla, maxillae, 114
Metatarsus, 114
Moult, 47, 51
Muffet, Patience (Little Miss), 65, 67
Muffet, Dr. Thomas, 67
Names, scientific, 116-119
Nephila clavipes, 39
Nursery Web Spiders (family, Pisauridae), 95, 138
Oecobiidae (family), 130
Oecobius annulipes (family, Oecobiidae), 130
Orb web, 123, 133
Order, 116-119
Ostearius melanopygius (Dwarf Spider), 136
Palaeocteniza crassipes Hirst, 15
Palps, 27, 114-115
Patella, 114